AIR FRYER COOKBOOK FOR BEGINNERS WITH PICTURES

by Timothy Durkee

Copyright 2021.

All Rights Reserved.

All rights reserved. No part of this book may be reproduced or copied in any form or by any means, electronic or mechanical, including photocopying, recording or by any information storage and retrieval system, without written permission from the publisher, except for the inclusion of brief quotations in a review.

Warning-Disclaimer.

The aim of the information in this book is to be as accurate as possible. However this is not a medical book, so it is for informational purposes only and comes with no guarantees. The author and publisher shall have neither liability or responsibility to anyone with respect to any loss or damage caused, or alleged to be caused, directly or indirectly by the information provided in this book.

Table of Contents

Introduction 3
What Can You Do with Your Air Fryer? 4
Top Benefits of the Air Fryer
You Need to Know 4
6 Must-Know Air Fryer Tips 6
How You Can Benefit from this
Recipe Collection? 7
Air Fryer Cooking Guide 8

Vegetables & Side Dishes 10
1. Classic Zucchini Fritters 11
2. Spicy Potato Croquettes 12
3. Black Bean Patties 13
4. Roasted Carrot Salad with Herbs ... 14
5. Sticky Brussel Sprouts 15
6. Roasted Beet Salad 16
7. Beer-Battered Green Bean Fries ... 17

Poultry 18
8. Barbecued Chicken Wings 19
9. Chicken Doner Kebap 20
10. Restaurant-Style Chicken Fingers ... 21
11. Thanksgiving Turkey Breasts 22
12. Chinese-Style Chicken Teriyaki 23
13. Greek-Style Keftedes 24
14. Classic Turkey Drumsticks 25
15. Italian-Style Chicken Drumsticks ... 26

Meat 27
16. Sticky Chuck Roast 28
17. Old-Fashioned Mini Meatloaves ... 29
18. Barbecued Rum Ribs 30
19. Spicy Fried Bacon 31
20. Pork Loin Roast 32
21. Classic Pork Chops 33
22. Restaurant-Style Burgers 34

Fish & Seafood 35
23. Crunchy Fish Fillets 36
24. Easy Fried Shrimp 37
25. Old Bay Fish Burgers 38
26. Holiday Halibut Steaks 39
27. Authentic Greek Calamari 40
28. Homemade Fish Fingers 41
29. The Best Cajun Scallops Ever 42

Vegan 43
30. Fried Tofu Cubes 44
31. Restaurant-Style Falafel 45
32. Tangy Corn on the Cob 46
33. Classic French Fries 47
34. Lentil and Mushroom Burgers ... 48
35. Classic Potato Fritters 49
36. Spicy Cauliflower Steaks 50

Snacks & Appetizers 51
37. Glazed Bacon Chips 52
38. Paprika Onion Rings 53
39. Mexican-Style Avocado Fries ... 54
40. Prosciutto Stuffed Jalapeños ... 55
41. Restaurant-Style Mozzarella Sticks ... 56
42. Cheesy Tater Tots 57
43. Parmesan Eggplant Crisps 58

Desserts 59
44. Mini Lava Cakes 60
45. Coconut Banana Muffins 61
46. Vanilla French Toast Sticks 62
47. Old-Fashioned Apple Pie 63
48. Polish-Style Strawberry Dumplings ... 64
49. Homemade Flaky Donuts 65
50. Kuih Kodok Banana Fritters 66

Introduction

I've been obsessed with healthy eating over the past few years, looking for the best possible diets and healthy cooking methods. I wanted to drop some pounds and save extra calories but not miss out on my favorite fast foods. Therefore, I decided to purchase an Air Fryer last year. It seemed to me like a good way to cook favorite fried foods without lots of oil. It turned out to be the best decision I've ever made! Besides being practical on a daily basis, the Air Fryer is the perfect tool for family gatherings and kid's birthdays. I've started converting regular pan-fried and oven-cooked recipes to my new machine and I was pleasantly surprised. They turned out great! Moreover, I have taken the art of frying and grilling to the next level. That's how this cookbook was created!

The Air Fryer is a unique kitchen appliance designed to fry food with minimal oil. It cooks food in a special chamber using the convection mechanism and super-heated air, hot air is the new oil! The Air Fryer redefines fast food with its possibilities for grilling, frying, and roasting, and warming your meals. You can prepare your meals just as you would in a regular pan but you can avoid extra calories and unhealthy fats. Plus, the Air Fryer always helps me to avoid that "there's-nothing-to-eat" situation on the weeknights. I always have frozen food such as fish fingers and breaded veggies on hand. On an actual day, I simply put frozen foods into the Air Fryer cooking chamber without thawing and preparing. Long story short, it's easy to make your favorite recipes in the Air Fryer, and it's almost impossible to mess them up. With all of this information, the next step is to put your Air Fryer into action!

What Can You Do with Your Air Fryer?

This intelligent kitchen machine radiates heat from heating elements and uses rapid air technology to cook your food with minimum or zero oil. Technically speaking, a mechanical fan blows heat around the space; consequently, the hot air circulates around your food at high speed, cooking it evenly from all sides, producing a crispy, golden-brown exterior and succulent, tender interior.

When it comes to the anatomy of this magical device, there are electric-coil heating elements. Then, it has a specially designed fan that distributes the hot air evenly throughout the cooking chamber. It also has a removable, non-stick cooking basket with a mesh bottom. As for the features of the Air Fryer, it has a Temperature control dial and Countdown timer dial. It means that you do not have to worry about overcooking or undercooking your food.

Most Air Fryers come with accessories, such as pans, grill pans, skewer racks, and so forth. However, make sure to use accessories that are designed to fit into your model of the Air Fryer. With all these accessories, the Air Fryer is great at cooking frozen foods, but it's also practical for from-scratch foods such as breaded meat and roasted vegetarian dishes; plus, it bakes extra-crisp cookies and scrumptious desserts such as pies, squares, and cakes.

Top Benefits of the Air Fryer You Need to Know

Healthy eating.
Thanks to its convection settings, the Air Fryer produces more flavorful food than conventional deep frying. It may change your eating habits forever!

Let's say you want to prepare French fries. Potatoes are good for you, right?! However, frying potatoes is harmful to your health. This process actually produces acrylamide; it is a chemical produced when starchy foods are fried at a high temperature and in deep oil (which was probably GMO refined or old). Acrylamide has been shown to cause cancer and inflammation. Researches have hypothesized that eating too much "bad" oil can raise the amount of harmful LDL cholesterol, speed up aging, and increase the risk of stroke. Avoid margarine, fake butter, baked goods, and processed snack foods at all costs. On the other hand, healthy and unrefined oils may become unhealthy under high temperatures. It is better to save them for salad dressings, right? Choose wisely and focus on ghee, butter, lard, peanut oil, grapeseed oil, and olive oil since they have a high smoke point.

Weight loss.
In my extensive testing, I found that The Air Fryer cuts calories, not flavor! Thus, instead of soaking your potatoes in a large amount of hot cooking oil, you can cook it with a tablespoon or two of healthy fat, and best of all – your food will not taste like fat. Studies have shown that air-fried foods contain up to 80% less fat in comparison to foods that are deep-fried.

It is often claimed that cutting down fats can help with weight loss – and that's true! Everyone should keep an eye on fat intake. There are two types of fat-saturated fats and unsaturated fats. Too much saturated fat can significantly increase the risk of heart disease and diabetes. Found primarily in plant oils, unsaturated fats in moderation are good for your health. You should focus on olive oil, coconut oil, avocado, and nuts. Nutritionists and dietitians recommend using non-stick pans to reduce the amount of oil needed. That's where the Air Fryer comes in! Just to give you an idea of the calorie content of the classic deep-fried foods. For instance, regular, deep-fried chicken nuggets contain 305 calories per 100 grams. Air-fried chicken nuggets contain about 180 calories per 100 grams. Then, onion rings contain about 411 Calories per 100 grams while air-fried onion rings contain about 176 Calories. The Air Fryer makes cooking at home quick, easy, and most importantly – healthy!

It saves your time.
With the Air Fryer, I can have lunch or snack within minutes. This is the perfect kitchen tool for me since I am constantly on the go during a busy work week. A considerable majority of these recipes can be prepared in less than 15 minutes. When I use my Air Fryer, a family dinner can be a reality any night of the week. The Air Fryer cooks much faster than conventional cooking methods. You can cook meat and seafood faster in the Air Fryer than you can in your oven. Clean-up is faster and easier, as well! No oil means no mess and no stress!

How does the Air Fryer work in practice? Spritz the cooking basket with cooking oil. Add the ingredients and set the time and temperature. You don't have to slave over a hot stove since the Air Fryer features automatic temperature control. The Air Fryer can also warm leftover foods.

6 Must-Know Air Fryer Tips

1. First and foremost, when using an electrical appliance, basic manufacturer's instructions should always be followed for safety reasons.

2. As its name implies, this Air Fryer cooking guide is intended as a guide only. The quantity, quality, and density of your food may affect actual cooking time. I always test my food for doneness before removing it from the cooking basket. When it comes to the meats, use a meat thermometer to ensure it is cooked thoroughly. High protein items such as meat easily become tough and tasteless when overcooked. You can cook food in smaller batches as needed. Shake the cooking basket or turn the food over several times during the cooking time. If you are not sure about cooking time and temperature, simply go 30 degrees below and cut the time by about 20%. It is easy to increase cooking time later but it is hard to save burnt and overcooked foods.

3. Never fill the cooking basket with more than 80% capacity. If you tend to overcrowd the basket, you're not allowing the Air Fryer to do its job properly. Consider a larger Air Fryer if you have a big family.

4. If you still miss traditional fried foods, mix melted butter with favorite herbs and spices to shake things up. The result is delectable vegetables with a crisp texture and fewer calories. You can also use a small amount of extra-virgin olive oil and add whatever aromatics you like (such as garlic, herbs, chili, etc.). A few drizzles of hot sauce work well too.

5. Make sure to grease the cooking basket. Use a cooking spray or silicone brush. This will ensure that your food won't stick to the bottom and sides of the cooking basket. However, do not spritz your food with cooking oil while it's inside the cooking basket; it can cause a sticky buildup on the inner surfaces of the machine.

6. Remember to preheat your Air Fryer. Simply turn it on for two to three minutes before using it.

How You Can Benefit from this Recipe Collection?

Are you looking for the best "make-it-again" Air Fryer dishes? Well, you are in the right place. My recipes are designed to help you create tasty and quality meals, from old-fashioned recipes to the hottest culinary trends.

In this collection, we'll explore an extensive range of dishes, from breakfast and snacks to vegan recipes and desserts. Each recipe in this collection includes a suggested number of servings, approximate cooking time, the ingredient list, step-by-step directions, and nutritional analysis. This collection also contains a lot of creative ideas. The Air Fryer constantly inspires me so I hope it will inspire you too! The best way to learn is from personal experience, so do not hesitate to experiment with your new kitchen appliance. Happy Air Frying!

Air Fryer Cooking Guide

CHICKEN	Temperature	Time (minutes)		Temperature	Time (minutes)
Breasts, bone-in	370°F	20-25	Nuggets	390°F	6-10
Chicken wings	360°F	15-20	Whole chicken	360°F	70-75
Game Hen	390°F	20-22	Tenders	360°F	8-10
Legs	370°F	20-22	Thighs, boneless	380°F	18-20
Legs, bone-in	380°F	28-30	Thighs, bone-in	380°F	20-22
BEEF					
Burger	370°F	16-20	Meatballs (big)	380°F	10-12
Filet mignon	400°F	18	Ribeye	400°F	10-15
Flank steak	400°F	12-15	Round roast	390°F	45-55
London broil	400°F	20-28	Sirloin steaks	400°F	9-15
Meatballs (1-inch)	380°F	7-10			
PORK and LAMB					
Bacon	400°F	5-7	Rack of lamb	380°F	22
Bacon (thick cut)	400°F	6-10	Sausages	380°F	12-15
Lamb loin chops	400°F	6-10	Spare ribs	400°F	18-25
Loin	360°F	50-55	Tenderloin	400°F	5-8
Pork chops	400°F	12-15			
FISH					
Calamari	400°F	4-5	Swordfish steak	400°F	10-12
Fish sticks	390°F	6-10	Tuna steak	400°F	8-10
Fish fillet	400°F	10-12	Scallops	400°F	5-7
Salmon (fillet)	380°F	12	Shrimp	400°F	5-6
Shellfish	400°F	12-15			

VEGETABLES					
Asparagus	400°F	5-7	Mushrooms	400°F	5
Beets	400°F	40	Onions	400°F	8-10
Broccoli	400°F	6	Parsnip	380°F	15
Brussels Sprouts	380°F	15	Peppers	400°F	15
Carrots	380°F	13-15	Potatoes	400°F	12
Cauliflower	400°F	12-15	Potatoes (baby)	400°F	15
Corn on the cob	390°F	6-10	Squash	400°F	12-15
Eggplant	400°F	15	Sweet potato	380°F	35
Fennel	370°F	15	Tomato (cherry)	380°F	20-22
Green beans	400°F	5-7	Tomato	350°F	10
Kale	250°F	12	Zucchini	400°F	10

FROZEN FOOD					
Breaded shrimp	400°F	10-12	Mozzarella stick	400°F	8-10
Fish fillets	400°F	14-20	Onion rings	400°F	8
Fish sticks	400°F	10-12	Potstickers	400°F	8-10
French fries (thin)	400°F	15-20			

Vegetables & Side Dishes

1. Classic Zucchini Fritters

Ingredients

- 1 teaspoon olive oil
- 2 medium eggs
- 1 pound zucchini, grated and squeezed
- 1 cup canned or boiled red beans, drained and rinsed
- 1/2 cup tortilla chips, crushed
- 1/2 cup oat flour
- 1 teaspoon baking powder
- 1 small red onion, finely chopped
- 2 cloves garlic, minced
- 1 tablespoon fresh parsley leaves, chopped
- 1 tablespoon fresh cilantro leaves, chopped
- Sea salt and ground black pepper, to season
- 1 teaspoon dried basil
- 1/2 teaspoon hot paprika

4 Servings 20 minutes

Directions

Brush the sides and bottom of the Air Fryer basket with olive oil. Whisk the eggs until pale and frothy.

Add in the remaining ingredients; mix to combine well.

Shape the mixture into patties and transfer them to the prepared Air Fryer cooking basket.

Cook the zucchini patties at 380 degrees F for about 15 minutes, flipping them halfway through the cooking time.

Serve on dinner rolls and enjoy!

Nutritional Information

Calories: 207; Fat: 5.5g; Carbs: 28.1g; Protein: 12.7g; Sugars: 1.9g; Fiber: 6.2g

2. Spicy Potato Croquettes

Ingredients

- 2 pounds potatoes, peeled and diced
- 1 large egg, whisked
- 1 garlic clove, minced
- 2 tablespoons fresh parsley leaves, chopped
- 2 tablespoons fresh chives, chopped
- 3 ounces Colby cheese, shredded
- 1 tablespoon butter, softened
- 1/2 cup all-purpose flour
- 1 teaspoon chili pepper flakes
- Sea salt and ground black pepper, to taste
- 1 cup breadcrumbs
- 1 tablespoon olive oil

5 Servings   35 minutes

Directions

Cook your potatoes for about 20 minutes until they are fork-tender; place them in a mixing bowl.

Mash your potatoes and stir in the egg, garlic, parsley, chives, cheese, butter, flour, chili peppers, salt, and black pepper.

Shape the mixture into bite-sized balls. Roll the balls onto the breadcrumbs and place them in the cooking basket; brush the balls with olive oil.

Cook the croquettes at 390 degrees F for about 13 minutes, shaking the cooking basket halfway through the cooking time.

Serve with tomato sauce, if desired. Bon appétit!

Nutritional Information

Calories: 404; Fat: 12.7g; Carbs: 59.3g; Protein: 12.9g; Sugars: 3.9g; Fiber: 5.7g

3. Black Bean Patties

Ingredients

- 1 tablespoon olive oil
- 1 ½ cups canned or boiled black beans, drained and rinsed
- 1 bell pepper, seeded and chopped
- 1 small red onion, chopped
- 2 garlic cloves, minced
- 1/2 teaspoon ground cumin
- 1 teaspoon chili powder
- 1/2 teaspoon smoked paprika
- 1/2 cup oat flour
- 1/2 cup cheddar cheese, shredded
- 2 large eggs, whisked
- 1 tablespoon soy sauce
- 1 tablespoon BBQ sauce
- Sea salt and ground black pepper, to taste

3 Servings

25 minutes

Directions

Pulse all the ingredients in your blender or food processor, leaving some larger chunks of beans.

Now, form the mixture into patties and place them in the Air Fryer cooking basket. Brush the patties with nonstick cooking oil.

Cook your burgers at 380 degrees F for about 20 minutes, flipping them halfway through the cooking time.

Serve on burger buns, garnished with your favorite fixings.

Bon appétit!

Nutritional Information

Calories: 389; Fat: 17.7g; Carbs: 39.1g; Protein: 20.2g; Sugars: 3.4g; Fiber: 10g

4. Roasted Carrot Salad with Herbs

Ingredients

- 1 ½ pounds carrots, peeled and cut into sticks
- 2 tablespoons butter, melted
- 1 teaspoon ground bay leaf
- 1 teaspoon dried dill
- 1/2 teaspoon cumin seeds
- Kosher salt and ground black pepper, to taste
- 2 tablespoons extra-virgin olive oil
- 1 garlic clove, minced
- 2 tablespoons scallions, chopped
- 1/4 cup parmesan cheese, grated
- 2 tablespoons white wine vinegar
- 2 tablespoons fresh parsley, chopped
- 2 tablespoons fresh cilantro, chopped

4 Servings　　20 minutes

Directions

Toss your carrots with butter, ground bay leaf, dill, cumin seeds, salt, and black pepper.

Air fry your carrots at 380 degrees F for about 17 minutes, shaking the basket halfway through the cooking time.

Toss the carrots with the other ingredients. Toss to combine and enjoy!

Nutritional Information

14　　Calories: 219; Fat: 15.1g; Carbs: 19.1g; Protein: 3.9g; Sugars: 8.7g; Fiber: 5.3g

5. Sticky Brussel Sprouts

Ingredients

- 1 pound Brussels sprouts, trimmed
- 1 tablespoon olive oil
- Kosher salt and ground black pepper, to season
- 1 teaspoon dried parsley flakes
- 1 teaspoon red pepper flakes, crushed
- 2 cloves garlic, chopped
- 1 tablespoon balsamic vinegar
- 1 tablespoon pomegranate molasses
- 4 tablespoons sesame seeds

4 Servings   20 minutes

Directions

Toss the Brussels sprouts with olive oil, spices, garlic, vinegar, and pomegranate molasses.

Cook the Brussels sprouts in the preheated Air Fryer at 380 degrees F for 18 minutes, shaking the basket halfway through the cooking time.

Place the roasted Brussels sprouts on a serving platter and garnish with sesame seeds.

Bon appétit!

Nutritional Information

Calories: 156; Fat: 8.6g; Carbs: 17.1g; Protein: 5.9g; Sugars: 7.5g; Fiber: 5.5g

6. Roasted Beet Salad

Ingredients

- 1 ½ pounds raw beets, peeled
- 1 tablespoon extra-virgin olive oil
- 1 tablespoon Dijon mustard
- 1 tablespoon balsamic vinegar
- 2 tablespoons fresh scallions, chopped
- 1 teaspoon garlic, minced
- 1 tablespoon fresh dill, chopped
- Coarse sea salt and ground black pepper, to taste

4 Servings

45 minutes

Directions

Toss the beets with cooking oil.

Cook the beets in the preheated Air Fryer at 400 degrees F for 40 minutes, turning them over once or twice to ensure even cooking.

Let your beets cool completely and then, slice them with a sharp knife. Place the beets in a salad bowl.

Add in the remaining ingredients and toss until well combined.

Bon appétit!

Nutritional Information

Calories: 119; Fat: 4g; Carbs: 18.5g; Protein: 3.3g; Sugars: 12.2g; Fiber: 5.2g

7. Beer-Battered Green Bean Fries

Ingredients

- 1 pound green beans, trimmed
- 1 cup beer
- 1 cup all-purpose flour
- 1/2 teaspoon garlic powder
- 1/2 teaspoon paprika
- 1/4 teaspoon dried oregano
- 1/4 teaspoon dried basil
- Coarse sea salt and ground black pepper, to taste

4 Servings

15 minutes

Directions

Pat the green beans dry.

In a mixing bowl, thoroughly combine the remaining ingredients; mix to combine well.

Dip the green beans in the flour mixture until well coated. Spritz the cooking basket with nonstick cooking oil and place green beans in the cooking basket.

Air fry the green beans at 400 degrees F for 12 minutes, shaking the basket halfway through the cooking time to ensure even cooking. Bon appétit!

Nutritional Information

Calories: 119; Fat: 4g; Carbs: 18.5g; Protein: 3.3g; Sugars: 12.2g; Fiber: 5.2g

Poultry

8. Barbecued Chicken Wings

Ingredients

- 1 ½ pounds chicken wings, tips removed
- Kosher salt and ground black pepper, to taste
- 1/2 teaspoon hot paprika
- 1/3 cup BBQ sauce
- 3 tablespoons butter

3 Servings 25 minutes

Directions

Pat the chicken wings dry with a kitchen towel and season all over with salt, black pepper, and hot paprika.

In a bowl, mix the BBQ sauce and butter. Rub the mixture all over your chicken wings.

Cook the chicken wings in the preheated Air Fryer at 380 degrees F for 20 minutes.

Serve garnished with lemon slices, if desired. Bon appétit!

Nutritional Information

Calories: 404; Fat: 19.4g; Carbs: 3.5g; Protein: 50.7g; Sugars: 1.9g; Fiber: 0.9g

9. Chicken Doner Kebap

Ingredients

- 1 pound chicken breasts, boneless
- 1 teaspoon peanut oil
- 1/3 cup hot sauce
- 4 medium flour tortillas
- 1 cup lettuce, shredded
- 1 small onion, chopped

4 Servings 25 minutes

Directions

Brush the chicken breasts with peanut oil.

Cook the chicken breasts in the preheated Air Fryer at 380 degrees F for 20 minutes. Transfer the chicken to a cutting board to cool slightly before slicing.

Cut the chicken breast into bite-sized strips. Toss the chicken strips with the hot sauce.

Fill your tortillas with chicken, lettuce, and onion.

Serve immediately and enjoy!

Nutritional Information

Calories: 355; Fat: 20g; Carbs: 18.7g; Protein: 24.2g; Sugars: 2.7g; Fiber: 1.6g

10. Restaurant-Style Chicken Fingers

Ingredients

- 1 pound chicken tenderloins
- 1 egg
- 2 tablespoons mayonnaise
- 2 tablespoons oat flour
- 1 teaspoon onion powder
- 1 teaspoon cayenne pepper
- Kosher salt and ground black pepper, to taste
- 1 cup seasoned breadcrumbs
- 1/2 teaspoon garlic powder
- 1 tablespoon olive oil

4 Servings 20 minutes

Directions

Pat the chicken tenderloins dry with kitchen towels and cut them into bite-sized pieces.

In a shallow bowl, whisk the egg, mayonnaise, oat flour, onion powder, cayenne pepper, salt, and black pepper. Dip the chicken pieces in the batter; coat well on all sides.

In a second bowl, mix the breadcrumbs and garlic powder. Afterward, roll each piece of chicken in the breadcrumb mixture until well coated on all sides.

Brush the chicken fingers with olive oil. Air fry at 360 degrees F for about 12 minutes, turning it over halfway through the cooking time.

Serve with your favorite sauce for dipping. Bon appétit!

Nutritional Information

Calories: 325; Fat: 28.5g; Carbs: 6.5g; Protein: 14.5g; Sugars: 2.2g; Fiber: 2.8g

11. Thanksgiving Turkey Breasts

Ingredients

- 2 pounds turkey breast, boneless, skinless, cut into 5 pieces
- 1 tablespoon olive oil
- 1 teaspoon poultry seasoning mix
- 1 teaspoon red pepper flakes
- Kosher salt and ground black pepper, to taste

5 Servings

45 minutes

Directions

Pat the turkey breast dry with paper towels.

Rub the turkey breast with olive oil and spices.

Cook in the preheated Air Fryer at 380 degrees F for 20 minutes. Turn the turkey breast over and cook an additional 20 to 22 minutes.

Bon appétit!

Nutritional Information

Calories: 313; Fat: 15.5g; Carbs: 0.2g; Protein: 39.2g; Sugars: 0g; Fiber: 0.1g

12. Chinese-Style Chicken Teriyaki

Ingredients

- 2 tablespoons olive oil
- 2 eggs, lightly whisked
- 1 knob ginger, peeled and grated
- 1/2 cup oat flour
- Sea salt and ground black pepper, to taste
- 1/2 teaspoon hot paprika
- 1 teaspoon garlic powder
- 1/2 teaspoon onion powder
- 2 pounds chicken breast, cut into bite-size chunks
- 1 tablespoon mirin
- 2 tablespoons agave syrup
- 2 tablespoons sweet chili sauce
- 2 tablespoons ketchup
- 2 tablespoons soy sauce
- 2 tablespoons sesame seeds

4 Servings

55 minutes

Directions

Pat the chicken dry and set them aside.

In a mixing dish, thoroughly combine the remaining ingredients until everything is well incorporated.

Brush the mixture over the chicken and place it in your refrigerator for 30 to 40 minutes.

Cook in the preheated Air Fryer at 360 degrees F for 15 minutes, flipping them halfway through the cooking time. Enjoy!

Nutritional Information

Calories: 474; Fat: 16.3g; Carbs: 23.2g; Protein: 56.5g; Sugars: 12g; Fiber: 2.1g

13. Greek-Style Keftedes

Ingredients

- 1 medium onion, chopped
- 2 garlic cloves, minced
- 1 small pita day-old bread, soaked in milk
- 1 ½ pounds ground pork
- 1 large egg, whisked
- 1 teaspoon dried oregano
- 1/2 teaspoon dried basil
- 1/2 teaspoon ground cumin
- 1/4 teaspoon ground cinnamon
- Kosher salt and ground black pepper, to taste

4 Servings

20 minutes

Directions

Thoroughly combine all the ingredients. Mix until everything is well incorporated.

Roll the mixture into equal meatballs and place them in a lightly oiled Air Fryer cooking basket.

Air fry the meatballs at 380 degrees F for 12 minutes, shaking the basket once or twice to ensure even cooking.

Serve the warm keftedes with pita bread and tzatziki sauce, if desired. Enjoy!

Nutritional Information

Calories: 504; Fat: 37.5g; Carbs: 8.3g; Protein: 31.5g; Sugars: 1.8g; Fiber: 1.5g

14. Classic Turkey Drumsticks

Ingredients

- 1 pound turkey drumsticks
- 2 tablespoons olive oil
- 1 teaspoon smoked paprika
- 1 tablespoon brown sugar
- Kosher salt and ground black pepper, to taste
- 1 teaspoon red pepper flakes, crushed
- 1 teaspoon onion powder
- 1 teaspoon garlic powder

4 Servings

45 minutes

Directions

Toss the turkey drumsticks with the other ingredients.

Cook the turkey drumsticks in the preheated Air Fryer at 395 degrees F for 40 minutes.

Serve warm and enjoy!

Nutritional Information

Calories: 244; Fat: 14.4g; Carbs: 4.5g; Protein: 22.5g; Sugars: 2.6g; Fiber: 0.5g

15. Italian-Style Chicken Drumsticks

Ingredients

- 1 ½ pounds chicken drumsticks
- 1 teaspoon hot paprika
- 1 teaspoon Italian seasoning mix
- 1 tablespoon honey
- 1/2 cup dry white wine
- 1 tablespoon Italia fresh parsley leaves, chopped
- Sea salt and ground black pepper, to taste
- 2 tablespoons extra-virgin olive oil
- 1 teaspoon Dijon mustard
- 1 teaspoon garlic paste
- 2 tablespoons tomato paste

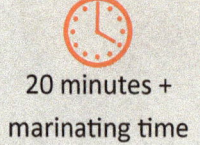

4 Servings

20 minutes + marinating time

Directions

Place the chicken drumsticks along with the other ingredients in a resalable bag; allow it to marinate for 2 hours.

Discard the marinade and transfer the chicken drumsticks to a lightly greased Air Fryer cooking basket.

Cook the chicken drumsticks at 380 degrees F for 18 minutes, shaking the basket halfway through the cooking time to ensure even cooking.

In the meantime, bring the reserved marinade to a boil in a small saucepan. Immediately turn the heat to low and let it simmer until the sauce has reduced by half.

Spoon the sauce over the chicken drumsticks and serve immediately. Bon appétit!

Nutritional Information

Calories: 367; Fat: 18.9g; Carbs: 8.9g; Protein: 31.5g; Sugars: 6.3g; Fiber: 0.9g

Meat

16. Sticky Chuck Roast

Ingredients

- 1 ½ pounds chuck roast
- 1 tablespoon olive oil
- Sea salt and ground black pepper, to taste
- 1 teaspoon dried rosemary
- 1 teaspoon dried thyme
- 1 tablespoon soy sauce
- 1 tablespoon fish sauce
- 2 tablespoons honey

4 Servings

40 minutes

Directions

Toss the chuck roast with the remaining ingredients.

Air fry the chuck roast at 400 degrees F for 10 minutes; flip the chuck roast.

Then, reduce the temperature to 360 degrees F and cook the chuck roast for an additional 30 minutes.

Slice the chuck roast into thin cuts and serve warm.

Bon appétit!

Nutritional Information

Calories: 395; Fat: 24.5g; Carbs: 10.9g; Protein: 33.3g; Sugars: 10.1g; Fiber: 0.3g

17. Old-Fashioned Mini Meatloaves

Ingredients

- 1 tablespoon olive oil
- 1 medium onion, chopped
- 2 garlic cloves, minced
- 1/2 pound ground pork
- 1/2 pound ground beef
- 1 egg
- 1 tablespoon Dijon mustard
- 1/2 cup full-fat milk
- 1 cup Colby cheese, shredded
- 1/2 cup tortilla chips, crushed
- 1 tablespoon fresh parsley leaves, chopped
- 1 teaspoon cayenne pepper
- Sea salt and ground black pepper, to taste
- 1/2 cup ketchup

4 Servings

20 minutes

Directions

Heat the olive oil in a frying pan over medium-high heat. Once hot, sauté the onion for about 3 minutes or until tender and fragrant.

Then, sauté the garlic for 30 seconds more or until aromatic.

Add in ground meat and continue to cook for about 3 minutes or until no longer pink. Remove from the heat.

Stir in the egg, mustard, milk, cheese, tortilla chips, parsley, cayenne pepper, salt, and black pepper.

Divide the mixture between ramekins. Divide the remaining tomato paste between ramekins.

Air fry the mini meatloaves at 380 degrees F for 10 minutes. Lastly, top them with ketchup and continue to bake for 5 to 6 minutes more. Bon appétit!

Nutritional Information

Calories: 515; Fat: 35.5g; Carbs: 18.2g; Protein: 32.3g; Sugars: 10.1g; Fiber: 1.3g

18. Barbecued Rum Ribs

Ingredients

- 1 ½ pounds beef ribs
- 1/2 cup tomato sauce
- 1/4 cup dark rum
- 1/4 cup soy sauce
- 1 teaspoon liquid smoke
- 1 tablespoon onion powder
- 1 teaspoon fresh garlic, chopped
- 1 teaspoon cayenne pepper
- Kosher salt and ground black pepper, to taste

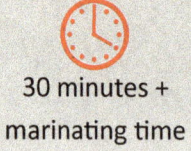

4 Servings

30 minutes + marinating time

Directions

Place all ingredients in a ceramic bowl, cover, and allow it to marinate for 3 to 4 hours.

Place the ribs in a lightly greased Air Fryer basket, reserving the marinade. Roast the ribs in your Air Fryer at 400 degrees F for 10 minutes.

Reduce heat to 330 degrees F, baste with the reserved marinade, and cook an additional 20 minutes. The internal temperature of the ribs should be around 203 degrees F.

Bon appétit!

Nutritional Information

Calories: 645; Fat: 50g; Carbs: 10.1g; Protein: 27.3g; Sugars: 3.7g; Fiber: 2.4g

19. Spicy Fried Bacon

Ingredients

- 1/2 pound bacon slices
- 1/2 cup tomato paste
- 1/4 teaspoon cayenne pepper
- 1/4 teaspoon dried marjoram
- 1 teaspoon Sriracha sauce

4 Servings   10 minutes

Directions

Place the bacon slices in the Air Fryer cooking basket.

Cook the bacon slices at 400 degrees F for about 8 minutes.

Meanwhile, make the sauce by mixing the remaining ingredients. Serve the warm bacon with the sauce on the side.

Bon appétit!

Nutritional Information

Calories: 259; Fat: 22.4g; Carbs: 6.9g; Protein: 8.5g; Sugars: 4.5g; Fiber: 1.4g

20. Pork Loin Roast

Ingredients

- 2 pounds pork loin
- Kosher salt and ground black pepper
- 1/2 teaspoon red pepper flakes, crushed
- 1/2 teaspoon dried basil
- 1/2 teaspoon dried oregano
- 1 tablespoon olive oil

6 Servings

50 minutes

Directions

Pat dry the pork loin using a kitchen towel; toss the pork with the remaining ingredients until well coated on all sides.

Cook the pork loin in the preheated Air Fryer at 360 degrees F for 45 minutes, turning over halfway through the cooking time.

Let the pork loin rest for 5 minutes before slicing.

Slice the pork into bite-sized pieces and enjoy!

Nutritional Information

Calories: 259; Fat: 22.4g; Carbs: 6.9g; Protein: 8.5g; Sugars: 4.5g; Fiber: 1.4g

21. Classic Pork Chops

Ingredients

- 1 ½ pounds pork chops, 1/2-inch thick
- 1 tablespoon olive oil
- Sea salt and ground black pepper, to taste
- 1 teaspoon paprika
- 1 teaspoon dried parsley flakes
- 1 teaspoon garlic powder
- 1/2 teaspoon onion powder

4 Servings

15 minutes

Directions

Toss the pork chops with the other ingredients.

Cook the pork chops in the preheated Air Fryer at 390 degrees F for 13 minutes.

Serve warm and enjoy!

Nutritional Information

Calories: 309; Fat: 15.2g; Carbs: 2.2g; Protein: 37.1g; Sugars: 0.6g; Fiber: 0.5g

22. Restaurant-Style Burgers

Ingredients

- 1 pound ground beef
- 1/2 pound ground pork
- 1 medium onion, chopped
- 2 garlic cloves, minced
- Sea salt and ground black pepper, to taste
- 1 teaspoon smoked paprika
- 1/2 teaspoon ground cumin
- 2 tablespoons barbecue sauce

4 Servings

15 minutes

Directions

Thoroughly combine all the ingredients in a mixing bowl.

Shape the mixture into 4 equal patties.

Spritz your patties with a nonstick cooking spray. Air fry your burgers at 380 degrees F for about 11 minutes or to your desired degree of doneness.

Place your burgers on pretzel rolls, if desired. Enjoy!

Nutritional Information

Calories: 428; Fat: 24.8g; Carbs: 8g; Protein: 40.4g; Sugars: 4.6g; Fiber: 1g

Fish & Seafood

23. Crunchy Fish Fillets

Ingredients

- 1 pound codfish fillets
- 1 tablespoon olive oil
- 1 cup breadcrumbs
- 1/2 teaspoon smoked paprika
- 1/4 teaspoon turmeric powder
- 1/2 teaspoon chili powder
- Kosher salt and ground black pepper, to taste
- 1 teaspoon garlic powder
- 1/2 teaspoon onion powder

4 Servings

15 minutes

Directions

Place the codfish fillets with the other ingredients in a Ziplock bag; shake until the fish is well coated on all sides.

Cook the fish fillets at 390 degrees F for 6 minutes per side; cook until your fish flakes easily when tested with a fork.

Bon appétit!

Nutritional Information

Calories: 168; Fat: 4.6g; Carbs: 7.8g; Protein: 21.4g; Sugars: 1.3g; Fiber: 0.9g

24. Easy Fried Shrimp

Ingredients

- 1 pound shrimp, peeled and deveined
- 2 large eggs
- 1/3 cup all-purpose flour
- 1/2 teaspoon garlic powder
- 1/2 teaspoon onion powder
- 1/2 teaspoon ground cumin
- Sea salt and ground black pepper, to taste
- 1 cup bread crumbs

4 Servings

15 minutes

Directions

Pat the shrimp dry using kitchen towels.

Whisk the eggs in a shallow bowl until pale and frothy. In a separate shallow bowl, mix the flour and spices.

In a third bowl, place the bread crumbs.

Dip the shrimp in the whisked egg; then, dip them in the flour mixture; roll the shrimp onto the breadcrumbs.

Spritz the breaded shrimp with nonstick oil and transfer them to the Air Fryer cooking basket.

Cook the shrimp in the preheated Air Fryer at 400 degrees F for 5 minutes; shake the basket and cook an additional 4 to 5 minutes.

Serve immediately and enjoy!

Nutritional Information

Calories: 208; Fat: 3.4g; Carbs: 14.1g; Protein: 28.2g; Sugars: 1.3g; Fiber: 0.8g

25. Old Bay Fish Burgers

Ingredients

- 1 pound tilapia fillets, blanched
- 1 cup breadcrumbs
- 2 medium eggs
- 1 small onion, chopped
- 2 garlic cloves, minced
- 1 tablespoon lemon juice
- 1/2 tablespoon Old Bay seasoning mix
- 1 teaspoon cayenne pepper
- Coarse sea salt and ground black pepper, to taste

4 Servings

15 minutes

Directions

Thoroughly combine all the ingredients in a mixing bowl.

Then, roll the mixture into four patties and transfer them to the lightly oiled Air Fryer cooking basket.

Cook the fish cakes at 400 degrees F for 5 minutes; turn them over and continue to cook an additional 5 minutes until cooked through.

Bon appétit!

Nutritional Information

Calories: 218; Fat: 7.8g; Carbs: 8.9g; Protein: 26.9g; Sugars: 1.7g; Fiber: 0.9g

26. Holiday Halibut Steaks

Ingredients

- 1 pound halibut steaks
- 1/2 cup pistachios, ground
- 1/2 cup mayonnaise
- 2 garlic cloves, minced
- Sea salt and ground black pepper, to taste
- 1/2 teaspoon red pepper flakes, crushed

4 Servings

15 minutes

Directions

Pat the halibut steaks dry using kitchen towels.

In a shallow bowl, mix the remaining ingredients until well combined.

Press the halibut steaks into the mayo mixture until well coated on all sides.

Cook the halibut steak at 380 degrees F for 5 minutes. Turn the halibut steak over and continue to cook an additional 5 minutes or until a meat thermometer reads 135 degrees F.

Serve warm and enjoy!

Nutritional Information

Calories: 218; Fat: 7.8g; Carbs: 8.9g; Protein: 26.9g; Sugars: 1.7g; Fiber: 0.9g

27. Authentic Greek Calamari

Ingredients

- 1 pound squid, cut into rings
- Sea salt and ground black pepper, to taste
- 1 large egg, beaten
- 1/2 cup ale beer
- 1 cup all-purpose flour
- 2 ounces parmesan cheese, grated
- 1 teaspoon granulated garlic
- 2 ounces breadcrumbs
- 1 tablespoon olive oil

4 Servings   15 minutes

Directions

Sprinkle the calamari with salt and black pepper.

Mix the eggs, beer, and flour in a shallow bowl until well combined.

In another bowl, mix the cheese, granulated garlic, and breadcrumbs.

Dip the calamari pieces in the flour mixture, then roll them onto the breadcrumb mixture, pressing to coat on all sides.

Drizzle your calamari with olive oil and transfer them to the lightly oiled Air Fryer cooking basket.

Cook your calamari at 400 degrees F for 12 minutes, shaking the basket halfway through the cooking time.

Enjoy!

Nutritional Information

Calories: 380; Fat: 10.8g; Carbs: 38.8g; Protein: 28.1g; Sugars: 1.5g; Fiber: 1.4g

28. Homemade Fish Fingers

Ingredients

- 1 pound tilapia fillets
- 1 large egg, whisked
- 1/3 cup all-purpose flour
- 1/2 cup bread crumbs
- 2 ounces Provolone cheese, grated
- 1 teaspoon dried parsley flakes
- 1/2 teaspoon dried oregano
- 1 teaspoon paprika
- Sea salt and ground black pepper, to taste
- 1 tablespoon olive oil

4 Servings

15 minutes

Directions

Rinse the tilapia and pat it dry using kitchen towels. Then, cut the tilapia into strips.

Then, whisk the egg and flour in a shallow bowl. Now, combine the breadcrumbs, cheese, and spices in another shallow bowl.

Dip the fish strips in the egg/flour mixture, then, roll them over the breadcrumb mixture. Transfer fish fingers to the lightly greased Air Fryer cooking basket.

Brush the fish fingers with olive oil.

Cook the fish fingers in the preheated Air Fryer at 400 degrees F for 10 minutes, turning them over halfway through to ensure even browning.

Serve immediately and enjoy!

Nutritional Information

Calories: 304; Fat: 11.2g; Carbs: 19.4g; Protein: 31.1g; Sugars: 1.6g; Fiber: 1.3g

29. The Best Cajun Scallops Ever

Ingredients

- 1 pound fresh scallops
- Sea salt and ground black pepper, to taste
- 1 tablespoon Cajun seasoning mix
- 1 teaspoon dried oregano
- 2 tablespoons butter, softened
- 1 garlic clove, minced
- 1 teaspoon lemon juice

4 Servings

15 minutes

Directions

Toss the scallops with the remaining ingredients. Arrange them in a lightly greased cooking basket.

Cook the scallops in the preheated Air Fryer at 400 degrees F for 10 to 11 minutes, shaking the basket once or twice to ensure even cooking.

Bon appétit!

Nutritional Information

Calories: 134; Fat: 6.2g; Carbs: 4.5g; Protein: 13.9g; Sugars: 0.1g; Fiber: 0.4g

Vegan

30. Fried Tofu Cubes

Ingredients

- 1 (16-ounce) block extra-firm tofu, pressed and cubed
- 2 tablespoons vegan soy sauce
- 2 tablespoons toasted sesame oil
- 1 teaspoon garlic powder
- 1/2 teaspoon onion powder
- 1/4 teaspoon ground cumin

4 Servings

15 minutes

Directions

Toss the tofu cubes with the remaining ingredients.

Air fry your tofu at 380 degrees F for about 13 minutes, shaking the basket once or twice to ensure even browning.

Bon appétit!

Nutritional Information

Calories: 194; Fat: 14.9g; Carbs: 5.1g; Protein: 11.9g; Sugars: 2.1g; Fiber: 0.7g

31. Restaurant-Style Falafel

Ingredients

- 2 cups canned or boiled chickpeas, rinsed and drained
- 1 small onion, chopped
- 2 cloves garlic, roughly chopped
- 1/4 cup parsley, minced
- 1/2 teaspoon ground cumin
- Kosher salt and ground black pepper, to taste
- 1 teaspoon red pepper flakes, crushed
- 1 tablespoon tahini
- 1 tablespoon olive oil

4 Servings 20 minutes

Directions

Place the chickpeas, onion, garlic, parsley, spices, and tahini in a bowl of your food processor.

Now, blitz the ingredients until well combined. Roll the mixture into small balls and brush them with olive oil.

Cook your falafel in the preheated Air Fryer at 395 degrees F for 8 minutes; turn them over and cook for another 7 to 8 minutes.

Bon appétit!

Nutritional Information

Calories: 204; Fat: 7.7g; Carbs: 26.8g; Protein: 8.6g; Sugars: 5.2g; Fiber: 7.2g

32. Tangy Corn on the Cob

Ingredients

- 2 ears fresh corn, shucked
- 2 tablespoons unsalted butter
- 1 teaspoon garlic powder
- 1 teaspoon lime zest
- Sea salt and ground black pepper, to taste
- 1 teaspoon paprika

2 Servings

20 minutes

Directions

Toss the corn with the remaining ingredients.

Cook your corn in the preheated Air Fryer at 400 degrees F for about 14 minutes or until slightly charred.

Bon appétit!

Nutritional Information

46

Calories: 211; Fat: 8.9g; Carbs: 33.5g; Protein: 5.4g; Sugars: 1.3g; Fiber: 4.4g

33. Classic French Fries

Ingredients

- 1 pound potatoes, peeled and cut into sticks
- 2 teaspoons olive oil
- Kosher salt and cayenne pepper, to taste

4 Servings

25 minutes

Directions

Toss your potatoes with the remaining ingredients until well coated.

Transfer your potatoes to the Air Fryer cooking basket.

Cook the French fries at 370 degrees F for 10 minutes. Shake the cooking basket and continue to cook for about 11 minutes.

Bon appétit!

Nutritional Information

Calories: 120; Fat: 2.3g; Carbs: 20.8g; Protein: 2.5g; Sugars: 1.4g; Fiber: 2.7g

34. Lentil and Mushroom Burgers

Ingredients

- 1 cup red lentils, soaked overnight
- 2 ounces mushrooms, chopped
- 1 small carrot, grated
- 1 small zucchini, grated
- 1 medium onion, minced
- 2 cloves garlic, minced
- 2 teaspoons flax seeds, ground
- 2 tablespoons sunflower seeds
- 1/2 cup besan (chickpea flour)
- 1/2 cup breadcrumbs
- 2 tablespoons vegan BBQ sauce
- Sea salt and ground black pepper, to taste
- 1 tablespoon olive oil

4 Servings

35 minutes

Directions

Drain and rinse the lentils. Cook the red lentils in a large saucepan of lightly salted water until tender or about 15 minutes.

Mix all the ingredients, except for the olive oil, in a blender or food processor. Shape the mixture into equal patties.

Now, transfer the lentil patties to the cooking basket. Brush the lentil patties with olive oil.

Cook the lentil burgers at 390 degrees F for about 20 minutes, turning them over halfway through the cooking time.

Serve on burger buns, if desired. Bon appétit!

Nutritional Information

Calories: 324; Fat: 8.3g; Carbs: 47.3g; Protein: 17.5g; Sugars: 4.7g; Fiber: 8.2g

35. Classic Potato Fritters

Ingredients

- 1 pound potatoes, peeled
- 1 medium onion, chopped
- 1 garlic clove, minced
- 1 tablespoon ground flax seeds
- 1/2 teaspoon ground cumin
- 1/2 teaspoon smoked paprika
- 1/4 teaspoon red pepper flakes, crushed
- Sea salt and ground black pepper, to taste
- 4 tablespoons chickpea flour
- 1 tablespoon olive oil

4 Servings
55 minutes

Directions

Place your potatoes in the Air Fryer cooking basket and cook them at 400 degrees F for about 40 minutes, shaking the basket occasionally to promote even cooking.

Mash your potatoes with a fork or potato masher.

Make a vegan egg by mixing 1 tablespoon of ground flax seeds with 1 ½ tablespoons of water. Let it stand for 5 minutes.

Mix the mashed potatoes, onion, garlic, flaxseed egg, spices, and chickpea flour; form the mixture into equal patties and brush them with olive oil.

Cook your fritters at 380 degrees F for about 14 minutes, flipping them halfway through the cooking time.

Serve warm and enjoy!

Nutritional Information

Calories: 167; Fat: 4.5g; Carbs: 27.7g; Protein: 4.5g; Sugars: 3.4g; Fiber: 4.2g

36. Spicy Cauliflower Steaks

Ingredients

- 1 pound cauliflower, sliced lengthwise through the core into 4 'steaks'
- 2 tablespoons extra-virgin olive oil
- 2 cloves garlic, minced
- 1 teaspoon chili pepper flakes
- 1 teaspoon cayenne pepper
- Sea salt and ground black pepper, to taste

3 Servings

25 minutes

Directions

Parboil the cauliflower in the pot with lightly salted water for about 15 minutes.

Toss the cauliflower with the other ingredients.

Roast the cauliflower steaks in the preheated Air Fryer at 400 degrees F for 10 minutes, flipping them over halfway through the cooking time to promote even cooking.

Serve with sauce of choice and enjoy!

Nutritional Information

Calories: 133; Fat: 9.5g; Carbs: 9.9g; Protein: 3.5g; Sugars: 3.7g; Fiber: 3.5g

Snacks & Appetizers

37. Glazed Bacon Chips

Ingredients

- 4 (1-ounce) strips bacon, cut in half crosswise
- 2 tablespoons maple syrup
- 1/4 teaspoon ground black pepper, or more to taste
- 1 teaspoon red chili flakes

2 Servings

15 minutes

Directions

Place the bacon strips in the Air Fryer cooking basket.

Cook the bacon strips at 360 degrees F for 5 minutes.

Now, turn the bacon slices over, brush them with the glaze ingredients and cook for another 5 minutes.

Enjoy!

Nutritional Information

Calories: 283; Fat: 22.5g; Carbs: 14.1g; Protein: 7.1g; Sugars: 12.5g; Fiber: 0.1g

38. Paprika Onion Rings

Ingredients

- 1 large onion, cut into rings
- 1/2 cup all-purpose flour
- 1 teaspoon hot paprika
- Kosher salt and ground black pepper, to taste
- 1 large egg, whisked
- 1 cup breadcrumbs
- 1 tablespoon olive oil

4 Servings

15 minutes

Directions

Pat the onion rings dry with kitchen towels.

In a mixing bowl, thoroughly combine the flour, paprika, salt, black pepper, and egg; mix to combine well.

In another shallow bowl, place the breadcrumbs.

Dip the onion rings in the flour mixture; then, coat the rings with breadcrumbs, pressing to adhere.

Transfer the onion rings to the Air Fryer cooking basket and brush them with olive oil.

Cook the onion rings at 380 degrees F for about 8 minutes, shaking the basket halfway through the cooking time to ensure even browning.

Bon appétit!

Nutritional Information

Calories: 143; Fat: 5.5g; Carbs: 19.1g; Protein: 4.7g; Sugars: 1.5g; Fiber: 1.1g

39. Mexican-Style Avocado Fries

Ingredients

- 1/4 cup all-purpose flour
- 1 egg, lightly beaten
- 1/4 cup yogurt
- 1 cup tortilla chips, crushed
- 1 teaspoon Mexican seasoning blend
- Kosher salt and ground black pepper, to taste
- 2 avocados, peeled and sliced
- 1 tablespoon olive oil

4 Servings

15 minutes

Directions

Mix the flour, egg, and yogurt.

In a separate bowl, mix the tortilla chips and spices.

Dredge the avocado slices in the flour mixture and then, coat them in the crushed tortilla chips. Brush the avocado slices with olive oil.

Cook the avocado slices at 390 degrees F for about 8 minutes, shaking the basket halfway through the cooking time.

Bon appétit!

Nutritional Information

Calories: 373; Fat: 25.5g; Carbs: 33.3g; Protein: 6.7g; Sugars: 2.3g; Fiber: 8.3g

40. Prosciutto Stuffed Jalapeños

Ingredients

- 10 medium jalapeno peppers
- 4 ounces Ricotta cheese, at room temperature
- 1/2 teaspoon cayenne pepper
- 1/2 teaspoon garlic, minced
- 3 ounces prosciutto, chopped

4 Servings

15 minutes

Directions

Place the fresh jalapeño peppers on a clean surface.

Mix the remaining ingredients in a bowl; divide the filling between jalapeño peppers. Transfer the peppers to the lightly greased Air Fryer cooking basket.

Cook the stuffed peppers at 400 degrees F for 15 minutes. Serve and enjoy!

Nutritional Information

Calories: 147; Fat: 12.2g; Carbs: 3.5g; Protein: 6.3g; Sugars: 1.7g; Fiber: 1.1g

41. Restaurant-Style Mozzarella Sticks

Ingredients

- 1 large egg
- 1/4 cup all-purpose flour
- 1/2 cup breadcrumbs
- 1/2 teaspoon garlic powder
- 1/2 teaspoon onion powder
- 1/4 teaspoon paprika
- Sea salt and ground black pepper, to taste
- 6 mozzarella string cheese
- 1 tablespoon olive oil

3 Servings 15 minutes

Directions

Whisk the egg in a shallow bowl. Then, place the flour in a separate bowl.

In a third bowl, mix the breadcrumbs with spices.

Dip the mozzarella sticks in the beaten eggs and allow the excess egg to drip back into the bowl. Then, dip the mozzarella sticks in the flour mixture. Lastly, roll them over the seasoned breadcrumbs.

Brush the mozzarella sticks with olive oil.

Cook the mozzarella sticks in the preheated Air Fryer at 370 degrees F for 4 minutes. Flip them over and continue to cook for about 3 minutes longer.

Serve the mozzarella sticks with marinara sauce, if desired. Bon appétit!

Nutritional Information

Calories: 302; Fat: 19.2g; Carbs: 15.2g; Protein: 16.6g; Sugars: 1.7g; Fiber: 1g

42. Cheesy Tater Tots

Ingredients

- 1 ½ pounds new potatoes, peeled and shredded
- 2 ounces cheddar cheese, shredded
- 1 tablespoon cornstarch
- 1 teaspoon flaxseeds, ground
- Kosher salt and ground black pepper, to taste
- 2 tablespoons scallions, chopped
- 1 garlic clove, minced
- 1 tablespoon olive oil

4 Servings 20 minutes

Directions

In a mixing bowl, thoroughly combine all ingredients until everything is well incorporated.

Shape the mixture into bite-sized balls.

Transfer your tater tots to a lightly greased Air Fryer cooking basket.

Cook your tater tots in the preheated Air Fryer at 400 degrees F for 15 minutes, shaking the basket halfway through the cooking time to ensure even browning.

Bon appétit!

Nutritional Information

Calories: 196; Fat: 5.2g; Carbs: 32.2g; Protein: 5.6g; Sugars: 3.7g; Fiber: 3.3g

43. Parmesan Eggplant Crisps

Ingredients

- 1 pound eggplant, thinly sliced
- Kosher salt and ground black pepper, to taste
- 2 medium eggs
- 1/4 cup flour
- 1/2 teaspoon cayenne pepper
- 1/2 cup breadcrumbs
- 1/2 cup parmesan cheese, grated
- 1 teaspoon Italian seasoning mix
- 1 tablespoon olive oil

4 Servings
35 minutes

Directions

Toss the eggplant slices with salt and black pepper.

In a mixing bowl, whisk the eggs until frothy; add in the flour and cayenne pepper and stir to combine.

In a separate bowl, mix the breadcrumbs, cheese, and Italian seasoning mix.

Dip the eggplant slices in the egg mixture; then, roll them over the breadcrumb mixture. Brush the eggplant slices with olive oil.

Bake the eggplant slices at 400 degrees F for 15 minutes; shake the basket and continue to cook for 15 minutes more.

Eggplant chips will crisp up as it cools.

Bon appétit!

Nutritional Information

Calories: 193; Fat: 9.4g; Carbs: 18.9g; Protein: 9g; Sugars: 5.1g; Fiber: 4.1g

Desserts

44. Mini Lava Cakes

Ingredients

- 1/2 cup dark chocolate, broken into chunks
- 1/4 cup coconut butter
- 1/3 cup brown sugar
- 1 large egg
- 1/4 teaspoon ground cinnamon
- 1/2 teaspoon almond extract
- A pinch of sea salt
- A pinch of grated nutmeg
- 4 tablespoons all-purpose flour
- 1/2 teaspoon baking powder

4 Servings　15 minutes

Directions

Microwave the chocolate chunks and butter for 30 to 40 seconds until the mixture is smooth.

Now, stir in the remaining ingredients; whisk to combine well.

Pour the batter into three ramekins.

Bake the mini lava cakes at 370 degrees for about 10 minutes and serve at room temperature.

Bon appétit!

Nutritional Information

Calories: 303; Fat: 18.4g; Carbs: 30.3g; Protein: 3.6g; Sugars: 20.1g; Fiber: 1.8g

45. Coconut Banana Muffins

Ingredients

- 2 ripe bananas, peeled and mashed
- 1/4 cup coconut oil
- 1 large egg, well-beaten
- 1/2 cup honey
- 1 teaspoon coconut extract
- 1/2 teaspoon ground cinnamon
- 1/2 cup coconut flour
- 1/2 cup self-raising flour

4 Servings
20 minutes

Directions

Start by preheating your Air Fryer to 330 degrees F.

In a mixing bowl, combine all the liquid ingredients. In a separate bowl, mix the dry ingredients.

Add the dry mixture to the liquid mixture; stir to combine well.

Spoon the mixture into muffin cups lined with parchment paper liners; transfer them to the Air Fryer cooking basket.

Bake your muffins in the preheated Air Fryer for approximately 15 minutes or until a tester comes out dry and clean.

Bon appétit!

Nutritional Information

Calories: 379; Fat: 15.2g; Carbs: 61.3g; Protein: 4.2g; Sugars: 41g; Fiber: 2.6g

46. Vanilla French Toast Sticks

Ingredients

- 3 medium eggs
- 1/2 cup heavy cream
- 1/2 teaspoon ground cinnamon
- 3 tablespoons brown sugar
- 1 teaspoon pure vanilla extract
- 3 slices thick-cut toast, cut into thirds
- 1/2 cup crispy rice cereal
- 1 tablespoon butter, melted

3 Servings

15 minutes

Directions

Thoroughly combine the eggs, cream, cinnamon, sugar, and vanilla extract.

Dip each piece of bread into the cream mixture and then, press gently into the cereal, pressing to coat all sides.

Brush the pieces of bread with the melted butter.

Arrange the pieces of bread in the Air Fryer cooking basket and cook them at 380 degrees F for 4 minutes; flip and cook on the other side for 3 to 4 minutes longer.

Bon appétit!

Nutritional Information

Calories: 299; Fat: 16.5g; Carbs: 28g; Protein: 9g; Sugars: 10.1g; Fiber: 1.1g

47. Old-Fashioned Apple Pie

Ingredients

- 2 (8-ounce) refrigerated pie crusts
- 2 cups apple pie filling
- 1 egg, beaten
- 1 teaspoon ground cinnamon

8 Servings

35 minutes

Directions

Place the pie crust in a lightly greased pie plate.

In a bowl, mix the apple pie filling, egg, and ground cinnamon. Spoon the apple pie filling into the prepared pie crust.

Bake your pie in the preheated Air Fryer at 350 degrees F for 35 minutes or until the top is golden brown.

Bon appétit!

Nutritional Information

Calories: 329; Fat: 12.5g; Carbs: 49.5g; Protein: 3.6g; Sugars: 24.1g; Fiber: 2.6g

48. Polish-Style Strawberry Dumplings

Ingredients

- 6 wonton wrappers
- 6 teaspoons strawberry jam
- 3 teaspoon cream cheese, softened
- 2 tablespoons almonds, chopped
- 1/4 cup confectioners' sugar

6 Servings

15 minutes

Directions

Start by laying out the wonton wrappers.

Divide strawberry jam between the wonton wrappers. Fold the wonton wrapper over the jam; now, seal the edges with wet fingers.

Cook your wontons at 400 degrees F for 8 minutes; working in batches.

Bon appétit!

Nutritional Information

Calories: 143; Fat: 2.9g; Carbs: 24.5g; Protein: 4.1g; Sugars: 5.4g; Fiber: 1.2g

49. Homemade Flaky Donuts

Ingredients

- 1 (16.3-ounce) can flaky biscuits
- 4 tablespoons coconut butter
- 1/2 cup brown sugar
- A pinch of grated nutmeg
- A pinch of sea salt
- 1/2 teaspoon ground cinnamon

6 Servings

15 minutes

Directions

Separate the biscuits and cut holes out of the center of each biscuit using a 1-inch round biscuit cutter; place them on parchment paper.

Lower your biscuits into the Air Fryer cooking basket. Brush them with 1 tablespoon of melted butter.

Air fry your biscuits at 340 degrees F for about 8 minutes or until golden brown, flipping them halfway through the cooking time.

Meanwhile, mix the remaining ingredients.

Brush your donuts with the glaze mixture and serve. Enjoy!

Nutritional Information

Calories: 393; Fat: 16.1g; Carbs: 58.5g; Protein: 4.8g; Sugars: 20.4g; Fiber: 1.1g

50. Kuih Kodok Banana Fritters

Ingredients

- 1 egg
- 2 tablespoons honey
- 1 cup milk
- 1 cup self-rising flour
- 1 teaspoon baking soda
- 1/4 teaspoon ground cinnamon
- A pinch of salt
- A pinch of grated nutmeg
- 3 medium bananas, peeled and cut into 4 pieces lengthwise

3 Servings

15 minutes

Directions

Whisk the egg, honey, and milk; mix to combine. Add in the flour, baking soda, and spices; mix to combine well.

Dip the banana pieces in the batter and then gently lower them into the Air Fryer cooking basket.

Cook the banana fritters at 360 degrees F for 10 minutes, flipping them halfway through the cooking time. Cook until golden brown.

Drizzle with some extra honey, if desired.

Bon appétit!

Nutritional Information

Calories: 363; Fat: 4.8g; Carbs: 73.5g; Protein: 9.8g; Sugars: 30.2g; Fiber: 4.3g